SPAIN
today

TEXT: **M. WIESENTHAL**
DESIGN: **J. OPISSO**

1st. Edition, March 1979
I.S.B.N.
84-7424-120-0

Library of Congress Catalog Card Number: 79-66160
This edition is published by Crescent Books, a division of
Crown Publishers, Inc.

a b c d e f g h

CRESCENT BOOKS
New York

SPAIN TODAY

Spain has always been like those women whose gait and bodies arouse passion, women that set alight the blazing fire of our desire. Puritans will call them sensitive and romantic, but really these are just epithets to apply to anything that kindles the heat of our senses.

Spain is a land with a rugged and sensual body, displaying a taut, bare skin. Travelers are attracted to it as sailors were captivated by the sirens of Mythology, who embracing them in their arms, led them with songs and enchantment into a new life. I believe that traveling is an adventure of the senses. Even the anthropologists agree with this when they say that man's development as an individual started when he became a nomad. We leave home in order to see, taste, hunt, feel and experience... And if a country like Spain has been able to attract so many millions of nomads (tourists) throughout its history, there is no doubt that the country exerts a deep and mysterious pull on the senses.

Spain is not a land of abstract ideas. Romanticism and abstraction come from northern Europe, product of the fog and grease. Spain means life, mass, images and flesh, concepts born of the sunlight and olive oil.

When a Spaniard is born an artist, he paints still lives like Zurbaran's, carves images of the Virgin like Salcillo's or writes in picturesque rhyme as Cervantes did. Even the famous mystics, like Santa Teresa de Jesús, has visions of God among the pots and pans, and when Velázquez portrayed Bacchus, he gave him the face of a Madrilenian "golfo" (rascal), and his old women are always depicted frying eggs. Great Spanish ideas always run the risk of ending up in the frying pan or the stew.

The image of a puritan and romantic Spain misrepresents the raw and carnal sensuality of the country. A Spaniard who is shy or hypocritical becomes addicted to the Spain of theories forgetting his body and its pain and fever. It is easy to love your mother if she is a tired old matron, but the Spaniards always feel they are the children of a lusty, arrogant, demanding country, and when they look at her, unconciously they are afraid of commiting incest, that terrible and aristocratic sin indulged in by the people of ancient times until Freud taught it to the masses.

When the life of the nation is enclosed within these dark frontiers, then the tragic image of Spain appears. A symbolist painter would depict this Spain as a dark but livid Lucracia Borgia, surrounded by jealous and crazy children who fight to the death to decide who owns her.

Spain is a female country, a matriarchate of virgin beauty. The Spaniard worships women. His veneration has been such that for centuries he kept woman prisoner in a temple of narrow-minded concepts and demands: reputation, jealousy and the home. Every Spaniard has a Virgin: Our Lady of Guadalupe in Extremadura; the Virgin of Covadonga in Asturias; the Mother of God of Montserrat in Catalonia ... The Macarena Virgin of Seville is the most famous of these feminine and motherly images of Spanish piety. Some people believe that the Macarena does not represent the Virgin Mary but was carved to inmortalize a beautiful and unfortunate Moorish princess who once lived by the Guadalquivir river. And who knows? Anything can happen on one of those warm and scented Sevillan Holy Week nights when the "Virgen de la Macarena" is carried through the city streets, a dark princess who draws forth waves of passion from the public. People scream, pray, cry and sing songs to her. The more hot-headed ones even adulate her as if she were a living woman.

"Isn't she gorgeous?"

"Yes, prettier and more honest than all of them; she spends all the night on the streets and returns to the temple just as virgin and honest as she left it."

The Spanish aesthetic ideal is always feminine. This is why one of the classical figures of Spanish literature is "Don Juan": A man who loved women so much, he wanted to be like them, borrowing their speech, honor and beauty, their laugh and their bodies.

Perhaps the Spaniard is the last survivor of the Renaissance. Stendhal said the Spaniard was the last distictive character left in Europe. Maurice Barrés more emphatically stated, "Spain is the last aristocracy in the world." "Even the humblest craftsmen," —said an amazed Italian traveler in the year of 1513— "preserve this haughty 'fumo di fidalgo' ": (give themselves airs).

Castilian vocabulary is full of expressions that reaffirm this arrogant sense of honor. Calderon says in this classical stanza:

Al rey la hacienda y la vida
se ha de dar; pero el honor
es patrimonio del alma,
y el alma sólo es de Dios.

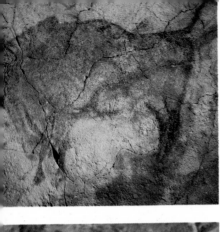

To the King estate and life
must we give; but honor
belongs only to soul,
and the soul only to God.

This concept of honor as a testimony of spiritual life or as the highest aristocratic virtue, has given birth to a very typical Spanish word: the "pundonor," an intimate sense of shame aroused in the depths of a man's dignity.

In order to understand the Spanish —and comprehend all the subtle shades of their language— we have to sensitively analyze these feelings. The Castilian language has its own vocabulary to convey certain moods that are an integral part of Spanish life. For instance, to express an strange and uncompromising desire they use the word "la gana"; When a Spaniard says "no me da la gana" (I do not feel like it) he is expressing the turmoil that is happening inside him on a physiological level, so that really he is justifying his denial by blaming his glands or hormones. The "gana" is a dramatized form of desire. A Spaniard always separates his vague, methaphysical, or idealistic desires from the vital desires that vibrate violently within us, like a craving for something, and only these merit the use of the term "gana."

The Spaniard, as the contradictory product of a mixture of bloods and ideologies, is sometimes a little sceptical. He only really believes what manifests violently —we could almost say biologically— deep inside him. His only reality is this material life. This is why great artists created some of their greatest works from mere objects as we can see in Velázquez and Zurbaran's still lives. This is also the reason why the Spaniard has always been a man of principles: his philosophy is stated just as if he were explaining to a physician the movement of his bowels. To tell a Spaniard that he is a man without principles is very insulting. And, truly, the history of the country has always been staged on the field of Great Principles. The Spanish conquered America moved by the principle of mission and conquest; the Moors and Jews were thrown out on a principle of religious and racial unity; the Counter-Reformation movement against Luther was motivated by a principle of faith in religious tradition. Almost all the great Spanish achievements have been made in the name of some principle or another, just like that immortal hero of Spanish literature —Don Quixote de la Mancha— who blindly followed on principle all the ideals of the knight-errandry.

This may be the reason why Spanish history has always been slightly behind the pace set by the other European countries. The Spanish always needed to work out their principles first, waiting for that elixir of "la gana" to start operating in the depth of their physiology. Thus, before the country would venture into the discovering of America, it had to spend several centuries struggling against the Moors. And it was during this endless war of reconquest that the prototype of the nobleman and the outlaw sprang forth, as heroes capable of conquering the world. In the same way, the Counter-Reformation was not really impulsed by the militia of Carlos V, but by the scores of saints and mystics who developed the Spanish principles of religion. Don Quixote also comes on stage late, (as usual), as an armor-clad knight, at a moment when European chivalry is already dead— late because a Spanish knight appears when he feels like it, meaning when he feels "la gana."

This delay in doing things got to be very well known when assistance of any kind arrived late: "Spanish assistance," it was called. An XVIII century historian remarked: "The English get things done beforehand: they are discreet people. The French do things on the way: they are proud and spontaneous. The Spanish only do what they have to do when the whole thing is over."

A people that work with so many principles cannot obviously, do things superficially. The Spanish have spent half of their history devising political systems and constitutions that were immediately rejected by a new generation with different principles. At present, for instance, Spain is trying to create new political schemes to live with, a new image better adapted to modern times. But just eighty years ago, the so-called generation of '98 —the men who saw the death of the Spanish empire in Cuba and the Phillipines— were doing the same thing: trying to figure out what was Spain. And a century before this, the first newspaper men of the Romantic Era, were searching for an answer to the Spanish crisis and the problems caused by Napoleon's invasion. I would say that Spain is a countinuous crisis and Spanish people are used to living at a constant and critical turning point.

And it is in these traumatic moment of restlessness and agony that the Spanish genius appears. Even the Spanish Baroque —the style that painted the Counter-Reformation— was born during the decline of the Empire: a farewell grimace of the Spanish bohemia, an aesthetic overstatement that fed and entertained a hungry people. Most of the Spanish artists from Cervantes to Valle Inclán have lived in such absolute poverty, that even their misery was Baroque. They were sculptors of the air, diligently elaborating subtle styles, always awaiting death. The Spanish bourgeoisie, that insignificant class made up of poor townspeople, never really appreciated art. If today Spain can boast one of the greatest art collections in the world it is thanks to its sovereigns. They were the only patrons of these artistic treasures, first acquiring them for their private collections and later giving them to the nation.

Uniting what we know as Spain has not been an easy task. Even the geography of the country —one of the most mountainous and rugged countries in Europe— has contributed to the lack of communication among the different regions. Successive invasions complicated still further this blending of races and cultures. The Gothic heritage is specially evident in the Castilian region, with its ancient feudal wars, its monuments and its meditative and simple spirit. The Greek and Phoenician culture, communicative and commercial as well as formal and civilized, settled in the Mediterranean region of the Levant. The refined and agricultural, aristocratic and universalist Roman history appears in Andalusia, a land that gave Rome a series of emperors and philosophers (Trajanus, Seneca, Lucanus), and contributed important figures to Islamic civilization (Abderrahman III and Maimonides).

But within this fantastic puzzle of traditions, there still exists a common history and a feeling of coexistence that has always been manifested in the best moments of Spanish life. Sometimes, one is led to believe that the Spanish people are exclusive and separatist; and to support this theory one could mention the civil wars —which are an experience common to all countries— or the expulsion of the Jews and Moors. But nobody remembers the long centuries of Christian and Moors living together in the same Spain. No one thinks of the Spanish Middle Ages, that period which was so cruel in other countries —when Jews, Arabs, and Christian lived together in perfect harmony under the reign of kings like Fernando III, called by his subjects "The Emperor of the three religions."

The long war of Reconquest against the Moors, made the Spanish respectful of foreign dignities and of the power of the opponent. The greater part of medieval Spanish ballads sing the glories of Moorish feats, and Spain is perhaps one of the few countries that preserves as one of its finest works of epic poetry, a saga whose hero is actually the foe's leader, the indian "Caupolicán of La Araucana."

This romantic and chivalric spirit also underlies Spain's greatest historic conflict. Spanish life has frequently tended to become a romantic play —with dangerous consequences. This may be the reason why XIX century travelers found in Spain nourishment for their most far-fetched and emotional fantasies. Barrés says: "If one considers Spain from a simplistic point of view, it seems almost as if this country is burdened by a parody of itself." From such concepts was created the Spain of Dumas, full of bandits and bullfighters, a strange, distorted portrait of Spain that Europeans consumed avidly. A romantic traveler asserts that Catalonians live subject to a constant craving for all things yellow, and depicts for us a cursed country —reminiscent of a poem by Baudelaire— infested by one-eyed cats who wander among the deserted cloisters of the cathedrals. This is the Spain that is to inspire the drawings of Gustavo Doré, "Les Orientales," and the opera "Carmen." Muleteers in country villages used to form gangs to attack foreign

Bullfight

Holy Week procession in Seville

A Potter of Chinchilla, Albacete

visitors who were on the lookout for any strong emotion. Nevertheless, this disturbed and incongrous image is also profoundly Spanish; nobody can blame it on the foreigners, for this is the very same Spain that gave us Goya's "Caprichos" (fancies), and Valle Inclan's "Esperpentos" (freaks). The absurd is the last showpiece of the Spanish Baroque.

There are few countries in the world that share this capacity for suddenly turning into theater, offering the most dramatic works. I believe we would have to go back to ancient times of early Greek comedy to find dramatists capable of creating a classical tragedy out of an everyday family quarrel. When a Spaniard does anything —whether it be taking a "siesta" (nap), making love to his mistress, or signing a commercial deal— he immediately makes a rite of it, stamped with his own, unique style. This of course, could be said to be the ancient heritage of all Mediterranean peoples. However, the Spaniard resembles that Andalusian beggar asking for alms: "Good Sir, give me a coin to buy me a hat, for the love of God!"

"And why don't you buy yourself some bread instead?" demands the bewildered tourist.

"Well... without a hat, how can I take my hat off to you?"

In Spain you have to know how to greet people; you have to master the language of the myriad subtle ways to say hello. You also have to be able to distinguish that subtle, almost ethereal something that Spanish people call "el aire." This "air" is more than just a matter of style: a cathedral, for instance, may be built in Gothic style and have an "air" of something sinister about it. A person can have an "air" of aristocracy around him. Any elegant or inspired gesture is called "airoso"; a rebuff is known as a "desaire," and in the epithet for a graceful person, the word "aire" takes the same prefix attached to male first names —Don Jaime, Don Carlos, Don Enrique— and becomes "donaire."

In my opinion, the air, that subtle architect of cloudscapes, is one more symbol of ambiguosness and Spanish Baroque. Even science is inspired, at times, by this strange muse: "Doctor, I have a pain in my liver. Could it be something serious?"

"Let's see..." (the physician fetches all the threatening instruments peculiar to his trade and examines his patient).

"Is it serious, doctor?"

"Well... this has the 'air' of being hepatitis."

In Spain "el aire" can mean all kinds of things, from an elegant demeanor to a sympton of hepatitis. Just as the beggar needs his hat, the Spaniard needs a language of clear-cut forms. So, when things do not

Basque dance

Flowered hoop dance (Santander)

Andalusian dance

"Corre de bou," Cardona

Pilgrimage of the Rocio, Andalusia

Pipers of Vigo, Galicia

Fiesta of Christians and Moors

"Castellers," Villafranca del Penedés

Falla, Valencia.

happen to be clear and definit... they have an "aire." This zeal for definition is patent in many ways. There are two languages, one conservative and one revolutionary, as also there is a poor way of life and an aristocratic way of life. Whoever dares to break down these concepts is called by a special word: "cursi." If your wear a large sombrero, with evident spontaneity to the Horse parade in the Fair of Seville, that is called elegancy. But if you drive your convertible wearing gloves meant for a racing car driver, then you are called a "cursi." One has to know in detail the rites and customs of the country to avoid falling foul of the "cursileria," (being corny).

The language of expressions, the plastic oratory of Spanish life reaches even the political world, sometimes with a tragic outcome. Thus, for example, revolutions usually bring countries a new order of ideology that is visible in social organization, civil rights, economy, etc. In Spain, however, revolutions are a totally different phenomenom: A revolution only brings a change in the colors of a flag, or some new

words in the National anthem, a replacement of one royal dynasty with another, or on the other hand, it may create a new way of greeting people. The frenzy of people greeting one another lifting one arm fascist style, or with the fist raised like the communists —was enough to embitter the Spanish Republican life of the 30's. The country at that time was going through an orgy of rituals in which the quality of a person or of his ideas was deduced from his gestures. One old exiled Minister of the Monarchy, Don Antonio Maura, answered a friend who was enquiring about his return by saying: "I will not go back to Spain until I'm allowed to greet people hat in hand."

This is Spain, an incognito even for the Spaniards themselves, symbolized by a grimace at life, or "the world's aristocracy" as Mauricio Barrés puts it. "Spain and I are like this, madam," says the principal character of a classical Spanish play after he has just lost everything for the sake of his lady. But of course he says it taking off his hat to her.

ANDALUCIA

Among the variety of Spanish provinces, Andalusia has had one of the greatest assignments in history, that of bringing forth the universal aesthetic types of this country. Its landscapes, dances, its temperament and turbulent and frontier history have turned Andalusia into the archetype or muse of Spain. Because of its geographical situation, this region is a products of many different bloods, traditions and ideas.

Andalusia resembles what experts call the "mother" of a wine: the residue that causes the aging of Spain's bouquet. Its people display that ancient wisdom, full of a gentle scepticism, that can only be acquired through long historical experience.

The most typical dishes of Andalusian cuisine, such as the famous "gazpacho," are made by squashing and grinding all the vegetables in the garden, the very essence and soul of agriculture.

Its wines are fermented and aged over years of improvement and patient waiting. Even the heraldic animal par excellence, the horse, is the product of an aristocratic crossing of breeds: Spanish, English and Arab. The blood of three civilized cultures and empire builders went into the breeding of the Andalusian horse.

The Andalusians are a classical people, lovers of beauty. They reject, on priciple, the artificial and the colossal. Their aesthetic taste is based upon natural things: flowers, whitewashed walls, even the body that draws curlicues as it dances. The only great monuments in Andalusia date from the time of the Romans, and time has slowly ground them down into an archeological "gazpacho." The ideal of the Andalusian aesthetic is always very simple. "Casi ná!" (It's nothing) they say when something touches their hearts. This Andalusian "nothing" has little to do with the absolute and desperate nothing of philosophers. For these Spaniards this nothing is the quintessence, the smallest possible amount of beauty condensed in the contour of a woman's waist or in the fragrance of a rose. Andalusians are not exactly a creative people. Their charm lies in how easily they can assimilate other people's inventions. For instance, the commonest elements of Andalusian architecture: the "patio" and the "cancela" (front door screen), are today a distinctive characteristic of the region, but they did not originate here. The "patio" is a part of the typical Roman house, and the "cancela" is a Renaissance ornament. The Andalusian, however, has been able to adapt these forms and plug them into his way of life. To the patio he takes his flowers, flower pots and he himself spends the drowsy summer siesta hours there. The "cancela" hears his poetic southern conversation. Lovers talk to each other through the cancela, letting this little screen filter the intensity of their passion. Just enough space for love to dissolve into the summer air, becoming a whisper, a scent, casi ná!

It has been repeated over and over that the Andalusian is lazy. But if one observes the Andalusian workers who live as emigrants in most large European cities, this idea loses consistency. It is not difficult for a people that knows the deepest secrets of the spirit to adapt itself to the rules and regulations of a bourgeoise or work-aimed society. A delayed industrial revolution has began in Andalusia lately, saving thousands of men from the heartaches of emigration. These are the demands of a modern society that is totally ruthless towards aesthetic feelings and lyrical contemplation alike. Andalusia today faces its industrial revolution imposed by modern times, but at the same time luckily it retains its authenticy and its spirit.

So, do not ask an Andalusian to forget his poetic spirituality or his oriental ideal of leisure. An Andalusian is always discreet in his work. He feels that to make an effort in life is like forgetting to take the price tag off a gift.

"What do you do?" asked an efficient surveyer to a peasant in the Andalusian countryside as he filled out a form.

"I don't do anything" answered the man, drying the sweat off his brow with a coarse, sunburned hand.

"You don't do anything, eh? ..." replied the bureaucrat in a menacing tone.

"Well, we make wine ... because wine makes itself, you see."

When you watch Andalusian countryside, covered with olive trees and vineyards, like a biblical paradise, witnessing man's work from sunrise to sunset until he almost becomes an old olive tree or a twisted vine, —do not think of hard labor. Because work gets done by itself, just as wine gets made with the passing of years.

Court of the Lions
at the Alhambra

SEVILLE

Maria Louisa Par

Partial view

The Golden
Tower

La Giralda

April Fair

CORDOBA

Partial view

Flowered narrow street

Typical courtyard

Synagogue

Plaza de la Corredera

CORDOBA, THE MOSC

Exterior view

Interior

Gate of San Miguel

CADIZ

The Cathedral

Plaza of the Catholic Kings, Jerez de la Frontera

Plaza de España

Algeciras

Castle in Puerto de Santa María

Algeciras

Arcos de la Frontera

MALAGA

Plaza de Queipo de Llano

Fuengirola

Ronda

Ojén

GRANADA

The Alhambra

Gardens and Tower of the Ladies at the Alhambra

Court of the Acequia, el Generalife

GRANADA

Carrera del
Darro

Purullena, a
troglodytic town

Montefrío

Pampaneira

Sierra Nevada

ARAGON

"What feeds two can feed three" goes an old saying that sums up Spanish courtesy and generosity when an unexpected guest turns up. Among rich people this would be nothing but a question of good manners, but the good manners of Spanish nobility do not come from the upper classes.

For this is also the custom in the humblest villages of the country, such as those on the rude lands of Aragon. Here bread is literally obtained from the rocks with great sweat and toil. But knock at any door and you will find hospitality. If two people can barely eat, three will eat much better. Could this be the meaning of the miracle of the multiplication of the loaves of bread and fishes based on love and generosity? The people of Aragon, at least, have understood it like that. This is the land that long sheltered the Jews and Moors when they had been expelled from the rest of the country. The result of this hospitality can be seen in the Moorish monuments "mudejares," the best in Spain. You may admire these churches whose spires rise up like minarets over the flat landscape. These are the strongest evidence in Aragonese history of that harmony between foreigners and natives, and between different religions and ideas.

Welcoming and warm towards peaceable newcomers, the Aragonese is, however, a passionate defender of his territory against any foreign invaders. When these people are threatened, they seek shelter in their own essence, in the deeper layers of their personalities where their best virtues are hidden. This is the reason why there were scores of martyrs in Aragon during the Roman invasion. They would rather die than surrender to the Ceasars. At this point they could endure anything: siege, famine, bombing... feeding on a curious manna produced by glands peculiar to a threatened Aragonese. Later, in the face of the French invasion, Aragon supplied the heroes of the most daring chapters of the resistance. During the War of Independence against Napoleon, an Aragonese genius, Francisco de Goya, depicted the tragedy of Spain. Goya is, in many ways, the archetype of the Aragonese mind. A sincere and rebel artist, he defied all affectation in art. He mastered, as few painters have been able, the disciplines of drawing and painting; as a good Aragonese he never retreated or panicked when faced with adversity. He stood firm and rebelled against artificiality and against any unnecessary adornment of life or art.

Aragon is built of brick, a basic and logical element which is the unity or cell of Aragonese architecture. The Aragonese reject anything that is not calid or lacks firm foundations: Even the Virgin Mary, when she appears in Aragon, is set on the top of a pillar. All Aragonese revere with deep devotion "La Virgen del Pilar," who is the patron saint of this robust and severe land.

Most of the country is dry and the farmer must work very hard to obtain his crops.

> There come the reapers,
> back from the dry lands,
> their ribs are all roasted
> and their hands are cracked.

These are the words of a "Jota" (the popular Aragonese song). The "Jota" is danced with arms raised, kicking the legs up the air, with a lot of energy and great involvement. This is a naive and spontaneous dance, without no deceit. Spaniards have a peculiar expression that is used to describe any spontaneous action, "Throwing the legs up," and this is precisely what the Aragonese do when they dance the Jota. However, this dance also has a kind of reserve, for the Aragonese is a little shy when expressing his inner feelings. Maybe he is afraid of being let down. He does not want to die, as old Goya did, of disappointment.

But no one should think that the Aragonese are afraid of death. Their creed could well be summed up in Quevedo's poems that nostalgically recall the old Spanish virtues, now forgotten in the decline of the Empire:

> That honored freedom
> when faced with an honest death
> never desired a longer life.

In that Aragonese legend, "The lovers of Teruel," the heroes die and honest death or die of love as Romeo and Juliet did. Archeologists discovered their tombs in a small chapel of this small Aragonese town, thus proving the veracity of this love story.

Close by the dry lands, cultivated with so much labor, we find the tilled soil of the vegetable gardens worked with love; the vineyards of Cariñema, the figs of Fraga, fruit of Jalón, the olives of Alcañiz... and on the slopes of the Pyrenees, the most beautiful parks and valleys in Spain.

Most of the industry is located in the large cities; Zaragoza and Calatayud. But the spirit of modern efficiency cannot change the human quality of the Aragonese. It is not difficult to build highways,

ZARAGOZA   El Pilar   La Seo Antigua   Plaza de España and Paseo de la Independencia

irrigation channels, factories, or generating plants in this land of solid foundations, whose ideals are symbolized by the shape of the "Pilar." (Pillar- or column which has given its name to their patron saint).

HUESCA

Mallos de Riglos

Valley of Ansó

Castle of Loarre

Valley of Ordesa

TERUEL

Tower of the Cathedral

Albarracín

Alcañiz

ASTURIAS

Everything in Asturias is intense and deep. This is a land of roots, caves, mines and ancestry. On the cliffs of Covadonga began the reconquest of Spain from the Arab invaders. A group of noble Goths, commanded by the prince Don Pelayo, faced the troops of the Calipha. This war lasted for centuries and its outcome was not to have winners or losers. The different races and cultures of Christians, Jews and Moors intermingled to form the soul of the Spanish people. Asturias played a decisive part in this historical confrontation to defend the Christian legacy. In contrast to Arab civilization and the Baroque expression of the East, Asturias represents the Christian civilization, the European heritage, the Romanesque. In Asturias, Romanesque tradition is visible on several surviving monuments, such as San Julian de los Prados, Santa Maria del Naranco, San Miguel de Lillo, etc.

In the times of the Spanish Empire, many Asturians sailed to the American colonies to settle there with their families and possessions. The matriarchal vocation of Asturias was what made it the foundations of the New World.

The Asturian is faithful to his country, to his loved ones and to his things. Several years after his departure for America, he would come back with his savings and spend them generously in his hometown. In this way schools, hospitals and the large mansions that are adornment of the Asturian valleys were built. All this coming from the "indianers," the emigrants to America.

Asturias is a region of intense contrasts. Its craggy mountains tower over the Cantabrian coast like huge sculptures of stone and snow. These sheer cliffs, carved out by thunderous falls, are the home of an almost extinct fauna: wolves, wild boars, deer, the same animals that the prehistoric man painted in his caves.

On the capitals of the monastery of San Pedro de Villanueva, medieval artists naively carved scenes from a bear hunt. One of the hunters —clad in goat skins—, challenges a wild bear and distracts it while the others stab the bear through the heart.

Deep are the green valleys that gradually descend to the coast, decorated with fruit trees and pretty hamlets. This is the rainy part of Spain, lavishly watered from heaven, with its villages set close to each other like a family at a well provided table. The landscape of the valleys is gentle, green, almost Franciscan in its simplicity, scattered here and there with little orchards, gardens and meadows all apparently belonging to one monastery. Peasants walk up the winding pathways with their horse carts laden with hay, and one can also see cowgirls here called "vaqueirines," their small feet clad in heavy clogs.

In the fishing towns, the atmosphere changes abruptly. In the air you can feel the constant threat of the stormy northwest wind the "galerna;" here we will meet tough men who are never afraid of any storm. The Asturian is used to deep waters and smiles at misfortune.

> Beneath your window
> they tried to kill me,
> little morning star,
> for coming at night to see you.

The "Asturianada," (typical song of the region) seems to smile gently even when singing of the serious side of life, death, love and life itself. It is sung in a deep voice with great feeling. The Asturian is likewise. His language is full of diminutives as if he were trying to reduce the importance of things. The typical light rain of Asturias is called "orbayu;" a thin drizzle that nonetheless wets both man and soil.

The real and genuine in life can be observed with tenderness and humor.

> La mia muyer morreu
> Enterrela en un payeiru,
> dexei una mano fuera
> pa que tocara el pandeiru.

> My life died and
> I buried her in the field.
> I left one hand out
> so she could still play the tamborine.

Such is the human philosophy of these valley dwellers. But there is another Asturias that drills down into the hills to bring up a wealth of minerals: copper, cobalt, antimony, iron, coal. Nature has been generous towards Asturias and thanks to this mineral wealth it has developed a powerful industry. A great part of Spain's heavy industry is centered in Gijón and Aviles. This great wealth is like the mighty voice of Asturias. It has its roots in a deep faith in the real true things of life and in constant surrender to the very heart of the earth.

OVIEDO

Horreo (Barn)

San Salvador de Valdedios, Villaviciosa

Capital of a column

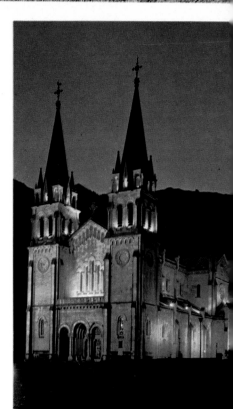

OVIEDO

Port of Gijón

The Cathedral

Lake of the Encina, Peaks of Europe

Beach at Gijón

Santa María del Naranco

Covadonga

Gijón

CASTILLA LA NUEVA

The name of Castile immediately evokes images of a proud, haughty, feudal and heroical land.
But these adjectives are more suited to Old Castile, the highlands watered by the Duero river. Of the history of Castilla la Nueva (New Castile) little has been recorded. This region of open landscapes is like a nude Spain with all what remains of the Spaniards and their country when bereft of all philosophies, decorations and vanity.
Simply imagine a proud warrior, with his shining armor, a crested helmet and a long polished sword in his right hand: this is Castilla la Vieja (Old Castile). Let us undress the mighty soldier and observe his physiology. This can happen in any pension of La Mancha, with its whitewashed well where the moon is softly reflected. The hour is grave, quiet and intimate, as are all hours in Castile. Our knight is slowly taking off, one at a time, his pieces of armor. In the moonlight that is reflected against the whitewash we can see the gaunt face, the bony body and the strong legs of a farmer used to walking over dusty roads. That distant, dreamy and patient stare looks familiar to us. This is the New Castile, the home of the nobleman Don Quixote de la Mancha, the land where the heroic adventures of errant-knights arouse humor.
When Cervantes looked for a home for his Don Quixote he chose La Mancha. He could have placed his hero in braver lands, for instance Aragón, or in Castilla la Vieja, or in the shadow of the Pyrinees. But his purpose was not just to present us with a traditional knight-errandry. His hero is an honest man, a daydreaming farmer, and a romantic. A Castilian from La Mancha. The characters surrounding Don Quixote are the everyday people of Castilla la Nueva: the boarder, the landlady, the barber, the priest...
In his adventures, Don Quixote is both brave and vulnerable. His skirmishes drive him not onwards but back home, and he dies comfortably in his bed, surrounded by his friends. He does not fall, like a hero, in the arms of an ideal Dulcinea. Rather, he dies in the arms of his landlady, like an old man returning from an ordinary day of work.
In Castilla la Nueva everything has this common domestic touch. The food is endlessly cooked in the coal oven under the attentive eye of the lady of the house. This is not a feudal and brave land: This is a modest world, quiet and patient. The Castilian was never an invader, nor has he many privileges; he was the trusty servant, a real friend, the quiet helper. His castles slowly dissapeared. Their

MADRID

Plaza Mayor

Puerta de Alcalá

Monument to
Cervantes at the
Plaza de España

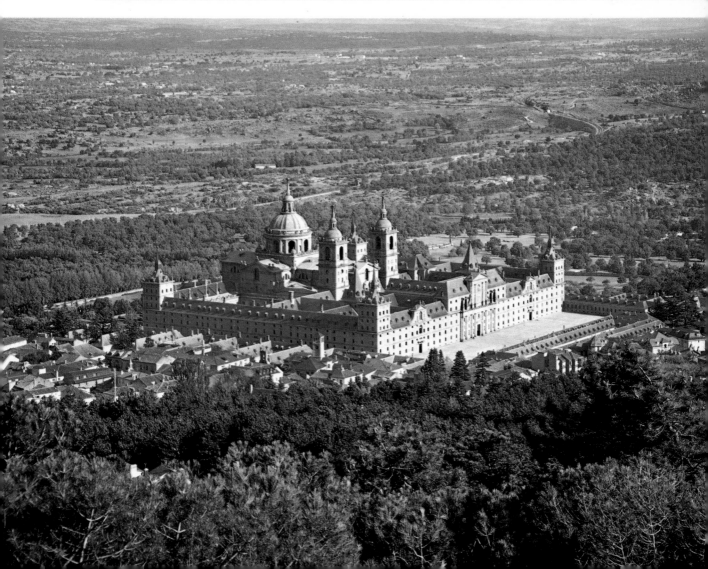

rient Square and
oyal Palace

as Cibeles
(The Cybeles)

a Gran Vía

oyal Palace of
ranjuez

Monastery of the
scorial

remains appear from time to time, as they are sold in auctions, devaluated and worth less than a car or a city appartment. The emigration has been strong in Castilla la Nueva. This is due to the scarce industrial developments of the region, in spite of Madrid's industrial zone, and several factories in Puertollano or Almaden. Sad, indeed, for a part of the country credited with fomenting a large part of the historical and artistic wealth of Spain as evidenced in Toledo, Cuenca, Guadalajara, the Madrid of the Asturias...

Towns are distant from each other, built by the shelter of a river's course, under the shade of a ruined castle or near the prosperity of the windmills. This is a silent land, of blue skies and thoughtful people. This is the heart of Spain bereaved of all adornments. It is generous and has transformed its bread into art, work into adventure and its own land into an open highway.

TOLEDO

Puerta Bisagra (Hinged Gate)

General view

The Cathedral

Transito Synagogue

El Greco's house

Typical windmill, Mota del Cuervo

CUENCA

The Enchanted Town

Cliff-hanging houses

Castle of Belmonte

Castle of Aragón

CIUDAD REAL

Gate of Toledo

GUADALAJARA

Walls of Molina de Aragón

Panoramic view of Sigüenza

Young nobleman (detail) at the Cathedral of Sigüenza

House of the young nobleman

Arabic Bridge

CASTILLA LA VIEJA

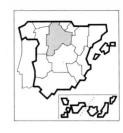

"It never rains to everyone's liking," runs a Castilian proverb. If this is true at a human level everywhere, in Castile it is also true as a metereological saying. I would even say that all kinds of life in Castile depend on luck or illusion. "Year of rains, year of wealth," says another proverb. Yet one more goes: "If it rains in St. Bibianne, it will last forty days and a week." Common proverbs in Castile very often have allusions to the rain. It has been stated, quite rightly, that the skies of Castile are large. One can see from the flat, dry, thirsty fields, that the sky is grander than the land.

The farmer here believes that in September a thin rain will fall enough to water his crops, that during the bitter winter frost the seed will take roots, that in March the winds will strenghten the plants, and that in April the rain will return. It will be followed by the warm summer that will ripen the ears of wheat, laden with their fruit. However, this is more a Biblical prophesy or a prayer to the god of rain than the true weather conditions.

Historians usually say that the Gothic and Germanic traditions brought by medieval invaders are quite evident in Castile. In this manner they explain the corageous and stern behavior of Castilian heroes, like the hero par excellence of the Castilian epic poem, Rodrigo Diaz de Vivar, El Cid. The story goes that before entering into the service of king Alfonso VI, El Cid makes the king swear that he had nothing to do with the death of his brother Sancho II. The king takes the oath at the church of Santa Gadea of Burgos, but never forgives his subject this offense. El Cid is then exiled, far from his family, and spends the rest of his life conquering lands for his ungrateful lord. The tale is a cruel and bitter biography: a life that depends on the winds of fortune, like the fields of wheat.

The German invaders left much of their heroic vocabulary to the language of Castile, for instance words like yelmo (helmet), espuela (spur), guerra (war), having a German root. The Gothic influence was also manifested in the best Castilian monuments. However, the heroic Castilian manifestations should not be looked for only in the influence of its invaders. These people possess the blood and ideas of many races. The patient and heroical root of Castilian behavior lies in the faithful surrender of man to the earth. To live off the earth was often more heroic than conquering Holy Places. In the time of Alfonso X, Castilian men were shepherds able to enjoy a tranquil life because of their productive herds of sheep. Their lands were

BURGOS

Monument to El Cid

Gate of Santa María
Towers of the Cathe

The Cathedral

Charterhouse of Mir

Frías

Pancorbo

Monastery of the Hu

Peñaranda de Duero

VALLADOLID

Façade of the University

Monument to the hunters of Alcantara

Plaza de Zorrilla

Castle of La Mota, Medina del Campo

crossed by the flocks heading towards the green north pastures. A rich wool industry was born, and the Castilian medieval fairs were equivalent to an earlier European Common Market, with traders from all the continent selling and buying different products.

Peace was always more profitable than war for Castile. But as the proverb says, that it does not rain to everyone's liking, the region was prompted by religious convictions to enter into a state of war. Castile was a land bordering the Arab kingdom and as a consequence was entangled in a long, draining war lasting for several ceturies. Later came the discovery of America, but all the riches brought from the New World were used to pay the expenses caused by these wars.

Hoping for rain, the Castilian man has been looking to heaven for a long time. From this inspired pose he has written some of the most celebrated pages of the world's mystic literature. Side by side with the epic poems of El Cid appears the loving prose of Saint Teresa de Jesus. This literature was written inside stone houses, in walled towns, amongst the silent towers of this high frontier land. The themes are always hope, true love, and faithfulness.

It is out of Castile that the universal Spain grew. Probably even Spain itself was the idea and work of a Castilian mind. Castilians wove the Renaissance rug of Spain out of the threads of many different cultures. The threads, when observed at a close range, are indeed very different. But in any case, they share the same rain and the same sky.

AVILA

General view

Gate of the
Alcazar

The Bulls of
Guisando,
El Tiemblo

Castle of Arévalo

SEGOVIA

Aqueduct

The Cathedral

Cathedral and City Hall

Castle of Coca

Alcazar

Castle of
Turégano

SORIA

Catalañazor

Castle of Berlanga de Duero

Portico of the Square, Medinaceli

Church of St. Dominic

Hermitage of St. Baudilio (interior), Caltojar

Cloister of San Juan de Duero

LOGROÑO

The Ebro River and a view of the city

Stone bridge over the Ebro River

Monastery of Santa María Real, Nájera

PALENCIA

Bridge of Puentecillas

SANTANDER

View of Puerto Chico

Beach at Santander

Castro Urdiales

House of Santillana del Mar

Collegiate church of Santa Juliana,
Santillana del Mar

Cantabric mountains

Laredo

CATALUÑA

Facing the mystic barrenness of the plains, appears Catalonia. It lies in the most northeast zone of the peninsula, a rich and plentiful land. This has been the Promised Land, the Mecca, for the poor people of Spain. Also, throughout history, Phoenicians, Greeks, Romans and Carthaginians shared the same idea.

The landscape of Catalonia, beginning with the green highlands of the Pyrenees, and extending to the fruit producing prairies of Lerida and the golden coast of Tarragona, is sweet and peaceful, almost sacred in its tranquillity. At times Catalonia seems like a sketch by one of the medieval artists responsible for the filigree work in the Books of Hours. It is clear why monks would choose this land of olive grows and vineyards to erect their monasteries. Even the kings of Aragon, like those of Catalonia, are buried in Poblet, right in the heart of this Promised Land. On the farms, men work their fields bearing monks' countenances, while the women knit or look after the poultry. Life is always in close contact with the earth, with its fruits and with the sun.

Without Catalonia, Spain would be naked or poorly-dressed. This is not a figure of speech, but indeed the literal truth, for Catalonia has produced for centuries the fabrics and garments that adorn all Spaniards. While other Spanish regions still concentrated on intricate tapestry handwork, Catalonia was setting up cotton factories and buying in England the machinery needed to develop a more sophisticated garment industry.

Many times throughout history, Catalonia has been the go-between for Europe and Spain. It could well be said that Catalonians are natural translators, men gifted with a special talent for carrying ideas and concepts from one language to another. These people, born of a rich blend of races and cultures, know well the secrets of the arts of commerce and communication.

Catalonia translates, trades and exchanges, but retains its sense of self, with its own language and culture. The Catalan was the first Hispanic language derived from Medieval Latin, and has always possessed a high degree of culture. Even Renaissance poetry was first introduced to Spain by a Catalonian poet, Juan Boscán, the constant companion of that famous romantic named Garcilaso de la Vega. Books of knight-errandry have a great story-teller in the person of Joanot Martorell, author of the "Tirant lo Blanch." Chroniclers of history reach peak heights with Ramon Montaner,

and Mystic literature is crowned by the works of a Majorcan author who wrote in Catalan: Raimund Llull. These are no minor regional figures, but universal names, the creators of real monuments of the spirit.

The Catalonian, like any Mediterranean, understands the universal meaning of things, but does not feel at ease with abstract or obscure concepts. These people love forms, color and drawing. Surrealism is at its best in the colors of Joan Miró or in the "Manierism" drawing school of Salvador Dalí. One finds still in Catalonia the classical tradition and the formal Greek philosophy which finds an exact worth and weight for things. Can there exist a more universal language than trade and commerce, where two different goods, two different objects, are exchanged according to weight and worth? A very subtle interpreter is required to discern the exact value of things.

In a land so sweet and rich men live like trees, rooted to the earth. In many Catalonian homes, even humble ones, you will find a genealogical tree on a wall, listing several generations of ancestors, like a seal of glory. There is recorded the history of a family that never left its land and that keeps, from generation to generation, memories of the "casa pairal" (the family's ancestral home) where they have their roots. "Among ruins of hanging dreams," —says poet Marius Torres, "and closer to the earth, protect us, oh Fatherland, the earth will never die." The Catalonian is a farmer, earthbound, a man of traditions and roots. The anthem of Catalonia is called "Els Segadors" (The harvesters). The background of the Catalonian flag is the color of a field of ripe wheat, turn gold like a good harvest. Even the best Catalonian painters have drawn landscapes. "Soc de casa pagesa," (I come from a peasants' house) can be read in the seal of a proud and noble Catalonian family. This is not a land of vast rural propietors. With the exception of Lerida, this being a more flat region, mountains cut the landscape and give it measure and weight. The Catalonian man discovers in the landscape a need for accuracy, detail and shape. This careful eye makes for great specialists in the scientific or technical fields which demand for skill and precision. Many Catalonians are surgeons, cartographers, chemists, engineers, etc. This

Taüll (Lérida)

attention for details is in itself a degree of civilization. Even the most insignificant things — a stone, a tree, a song — are treated with interest and love in Catalonia.

On the coast, the love for the earth is greater than that for the ocean. This is perhaps the reason why Catalonian sailors are more dedicated to coastal trade and fishing, rather than that of the open sea. There was once a historic event that led Catalonian sailors to Constantinople, but this was just a short term adventure. Homesickness and pain are felt by a Catalonian when he is far from his soil on the open sea.

With the advance of the industrial revolution, Catalonia faced the dangers of a newly inhuman society, divided into hostile classes and bled by labor conflicts. A huge emigrant population, that came from all parts of Spain, settled down in Barcelona and vicinities, close to the industrial belt.

These were people without a land, working in factories which preyed upon this cheap labor. The great problem of Catalonia was how to assimilate these people, to reconcile them to its way of life and its land. During the tragic frenzy of this mass immigration, sociologists and politicians from all Spain proposed diverse plans to aid assimilation. However, the Catalonian solution was the easiest. Today, many of these immigrant people have, thanks to work given them, a house and a vegetable garden, a piece of the land of Catalonia.

Even in the most tragic moments of his history, the Catalonian proves to be a patient, stubborn and optimistic man. All his problems find a solution in unity. His method is not revolution — that insane three hundred and sixty degree turn that leaves things worst than they were, — but evolution. The tree grows and bears fruit when remains attached to its roots.

BARCELONA

The Cathedral in the Gothic Quarter

Plaza de Cataluña

Rambla of the Flowers

The Palace of Music of Catalonia

The Sagrada Familia (The Holy Family) —Gaudí—

General view as seen from the port

Monastery of Our Lady of Montserrat

Monastery of St. Cugat

Sitges

TARRAGONA

Arch of Bara

Gate of the Roman wall

Monastery of Poblet

Iberian and Roman walls

GERONA

The Cathedral

Cadaqués

Costa Brava

Baget

Llivia

EXTREMADURA

Extremadura, as its name hints, is the extreme point, the border of Spain. The greater part of its history passed amidst the opposing interests of Arabs and Christians, Portuguese and Spaniards, and of princes and nobleman who settled their quarrels in this distant and open land. The peasant of Extremadura, tough and hard, as well as sincere and self-sacrificing, has seen it all. Things have passed him by, such as different cultures, various invaders, fluctuating wealth and erradic harvests.

The Romans built Merida as the capital of their large Lusitanian province. They laid out bridges and walkways, and adorned the city with monuments and theaters. Later came decay and ruin and things faded away, as in a fairy tale.

It seems that history always is swift and hectic in Extremadura, like a hound running on the plains or as the waters of the Tajo river run to the ocean. It is sad that in this same manner the Extremenian men took to emigration for adventure's sake. The beautiful landscape of Extremadura, filled with olive and oak trees, brown clay and golden wheat, did not produce enough to be able to feed its people. A large number of the fields were used to feed the transient herds of cattle, led by nomadic cowboys. One of these shepherds, the illegitimate child of a noble family, would almost without help, accomplish the incredible conquest of Peru. Accompanied by a handful of starved and desperate men, he conquered the throne of the kingdom of Gold and entered into the forbidden sanctuary of the Inca. Another man of Extremadura, Hernán Cortés, conquered the capital of the Aztec empire. Those who have read the chronicles of this conquest will understand how an Extremenian, no matter how humble he is, may be taken for a god. When the Aztec priests saw Cortés and his men, the priests, used to communicating with heavenly powers, believed that they were facing one of their gods. This was Tetzalcoatl, a mythical figure predicted to appear with a new civilization. Another famous son of Extremadura was Nuñez de Balboa, who discovered the Pacific Ocean. This was possible because he and his men carried their ships overland across the Isthmus of Panamá.

It has been said that the Spanish brought to the homeland endless amounts of American gold and in turn they sent to America their men. Extremadura knows well this chapter of History which has no title in the world of politics: the sending of its own blood to foreign and unknown lands.

CACERES

Monastery of Guadalupe

Trujillo

BADAJOZ

Walls in Mérida

Roman Theater

Medellín

Extremadura has always been the most nomadic area of Spain. Carlos V ended his days in the sweet solitude of the Monastery of Yuste, accompanied by the comforts of his station. So was the fate of Extremadura: to welcome travelers, even emperors seeking a place to die.

Pilgrims bound for that jewel of Spanish art, the Monastery of Guadalupe, also came to the lands of this province. Amongst them were Columbus, Cervantes, Felipe II and Zurbaran, the artist who has so well depicted the transience, brief, illusory quality of life.

We see now that the people of Extremadura have always been inclined more to individual, than group behavior. What the Extremenian wanted was to make his own history, not that of others. Towards this end it was necessary to adapt the economy of the region to innovations. Recently new roads and artificial lakes, channels and ways of communication have been created. With better irrigation techniques vast lands were newly utilized for cultivation. Slowly, a different, less nomadic image of Extremadura is appearing.

There is no doubt that there is still history to be made. But today's man of Extremadura is making history on his own land.

GALICIA

For many centuries Galicia was considered to be the "Finis Terrae," the most western, and thus, most far point on earth. But these humid and forested regions were more than a geographical landmark: they comprised the gateway to unknown places, the border land to mystery. A Roman historian tells us how the Roman Legion watched with "sacred fright" an ocean sunset at that magic moment when the sun disappears into the horizon. Ceasar's soldiers felt lost in this mysterious land, inhabited by strange gods hidding in the thick forests. Accostumed as they were to the bright sunny skies of Italy drawing a sharp outline to things, they believed that in Galicia thay had crossed the river of Oblivion, the mythical Leteo river, that as legend went, turned men into homeless vagabonds.

The air and light in Galicia are full of magic. Sometimes, on a foggy morning we see how words uttered by an old woman materialize into solid matter as she speaks them. In evening shadows peasants are said to have seen quite often a strange procession passing the hills: it is the "Holy Company," the fraternity of suffering souls that cannot find rest. Things both begin and end in Galicia, hot-water springs, rivers with gold pebbles, palaces with buried treasure...

There are regions of Spain which mine oil, nickel and iron from the earth, but in Galicia it is different. What is mined here is not ores but mystery, heavy with magic and miracles. From the depths of Galicia rise midgets, Moors, treasure keepers, dogs barking on the waves of the ocean and wandering spirits. Once, the apostle St. James appeared from the earth beheaded. Where the apparition took place is now the beautiful church of Compostela, that has attracted thousands of pilgrims from all over the world. The famous road of St. James (Santiago), was one of the most important conductors of culture in the Middle Ages. The church and its pilgrims forged new links between the peoples of Europe. Even today one finds the hospitals, churches, convents and hermitages of the road of St. James, built by the pilgrims during their long walk of piety.

The miraculous Galician soil was eagerly and well used by monks for raising their monasteries, some of which are prime samples of Romanesque architecture.

And the ocean is just as miraculous as the earth in Galicia. Often the fishermen went to work in their

ancient "dornas" and came back with the mental image of Christ walking on the water.

The Galicians enjoy inhabiting the "Finis Terrae" living in a lyrical and poetic land, which produces miracles amidst a prosaic harvest of vegetables. At heart they are people laden with history, a culture and good humor. They speak a gentle language, a derivative of the Roman legionaries' Latin now turned poetic. When they emigrate far away from their native land, they fall ill with "morriña": a kind of melancholy for the miracle, a homesickness for the mysterious.

In order to believe in miracles, the Galician needs to feed on solid food. If you ever go to the "romeria" (pilgrimage) of Santa Marta of Ribarteme, you will enjoy an incredible spectacle; Pallbearers carrying coffins laden with those previously sick people recently cured by St. Marta. At the end of the procession, the "dead" rise from their coffins, and like Lazarus, leave with their families to eat delicious meat pies accompanied by the wine of the region. There is, without a doubt, a reality to life in Galicia. There is also, — beware statistics fans! — a powerful fishing-related industry, including canneries, shipyards, etc. But still this is not enough to feed Galicia, unless a miracle occurs.

LA CORUÑA

Santiago de
Compostela

Monastery of
San Martin
Pinario, Santiago
de Compostela

Port and Marina
Avenue

LUGO

Aerial view
including the
Cathedral

City Hall

Port of Ribadeo

Roman Bridge
over the Miño
River

Vicedo

ORENSE

''Cruceiro'' and
''Horreo'' in Ribas
de Sil

The Miño River
at Orense

PONTEVEDRA

Plaza de la Leña

View of the city and the Vigo estuary

Portonovo

Selecting wild horses to be
saddle-broken, Oya

Tuy

The Pontevedra estuary

LEON

If we were to ask an astrologer for the defining characteristics of the Zodiac sign Leo, he would tell us that Leo is proud, powerful, energetic, strong and high-minded. These are, more or less, the same characteristics describing the people of the three provinces comprising the region of Leon.

From its beginning, the history of Leon has been of a warlike, militarystic nature. Here was born a shepherd named Viriato, who waged guerrilla warfare against the Roman legions. El Cid fought here in the name of his king. And in the small town of Salamanca, Bernardo del Carpio was born, the knight who, as legend goes, defeated the brave Roland in Roncesvalles. The historic duel of Paso Honroso took place by the shores of the Orbigo river. In this duel, for thirty days and thirty nights, the lovesick knight Suero de Quiñones challenged all the other knights of Europe in order to prove his honor.

Even the saints of Leon were corageous and brave. It is said that St. John (San Juan) of Sahagun, the miracle performing patron saint of Salamanca, withstood while standing up, the charge of a mad bull who was threatening the people of the city. The kingdom of Leon was independent for many centuries. But because of its geography, centered amidst Extremadura, Asturias, Portugal and Castile, it was a vulnerable land. Several roads crossed the entire region. Leon has flat lands, with vineyards and wheat abrubtly rising to the European Peaks. In its swift and fresh rivers are delicious trout. In the villages by the mountains are fine seasoned sausages. This is a pastoral and restful land that calls for meditation and a slow pace. However, Almanzor the Moor crossed this land running like crazy and leaving a trail of total destruction. The pilgrims walked across here in slow stretches on the road of Leon, towards the route of St. James; history has preserved the monuments these pilgrims left behind. Even literary characters, like the blindman's guide "Lazarillo de Tormes" are place amongst these roads.

The land of Leon is not poor. It has a wealthy subsoil that contains uranium, wolfram, iron and soft coal. There are also cattle, abundant game, as well as large gardens growing chickpeas, long beans, wine grapes and wheat. Famous wool is woven in Bejar, fabric renowned as early as the XV century. What nature forgot to put in Leon, man has added. For instance, two of the nicest cities of Spain, Salamanca (once the university of Europe) and the city of Leon, (with its great cathedrals and

impressive fortresses) are of this province. Leon is a land of pilgrims and shepherds as well as a land of warriors. Their concept of war was that shared by medieval knights, based on honor and love. Those courteous men "hidalgos" of the past — knights, monks, noblemen —, never surrendered their aristocratic qualities, though today you can find them as peasants, shepherds or simple workers of this dark industrial society.

LEON

The Cathedral

The San Marcos Hostal

Gaudi Episcopal Palace, Astorga

Castle of Valencia de Don Juan

The Cathedral of Astorga

Sahagún

Inn of Valdón, Peaks of Europe

Market day at the Plaza Mayor

ZAMORA

Partial view

SALAMANCA

The Cathedral and Bridge over the
Tormes River

Casa de las Conchas (House of Shells)

Facade of the University

The New Cathedral

MURCIA

The region of Murcia lies in the southeast part of Spain, between Valencia, Aragon, Castile and Andalusia. So centered, it seems like most diverse forces pull her in all directions. Perhaps this is an explanation for the extensive emigration from Murcia. Murcians go to Madrid, Barcelona, Valencia... looking for work and an elusive dream of prosperity. Always something of a foreigner, his Levantine and Mediterranean temperament is reinforced when in Castile; his Castilian blood is stronger when he lives in Catalonia; and he is a dreamer in Valencia.

The land of Murcia also is like this: its vegetable gardens are like those of Valencia; the prairies get confused with those of La Mancha, and in the south it looks like Andalusia. In the gardens the water flows gently, and in the dry lands one smells the scent of Rosemary, the tiny herbs fighting the battle against thirst and wind.

Under this direct, strong and harsh sun, shadows are lost. Murcia is no poorer that the rest of Spain. The port of Cartagena, by its volume of exports — so uncontrolled! — is one of the most importants in Spain. An even more important oil refinery, one of the biggers in Europe, functions in Escombreras. Mighty rivers and vast swamps water Murcian crops. However, things seem not unified.

The Arabs accomplished amazing feats of irrigation in the aridity of Murcia, and brought about regulation of agriculture. But when the orders to expel the Moors from Spain came, —again the destructive force! — the economy of Murcia received a severe blow. After the Moors came the Christians who built castles later destroyed by the wind. Great ideas and ambitious undertakings were lost. Perhaps the mayor characteristic of the people of Murcia is their care in doing simple things. Salzillo was from Murcia, the famous craftsman of wonderful religious images. His carvings still enjoy mass popularity and devotion during the solemn procession of the Holy Week in Murcia. The inventors of the helicopter and the submarine, La Cierva and Peral, respectively, were sons of Murcia. Working with such simple things as the chisel, the spade, and building clay, Murcians raised monuments for eternity in the same way that the Rosemary smells, that the water sings.

MURCIA

Persian wheel in Alcantarilla

Facade of the Cathedral

Church of Santa Cruz, Caravaca

Caravaca

Vega Alta del Segura, Ojós

ALBACETE

City Hall of Chinchilla

Castle of Almansa

NAVARRA

In order to explain the soul and history of Navarra I would have to be a juggler, or a wandering minstrel with tales of love and war. In the lands of Navarra history is more than a simple compilation of things past; it is an ensuing adventure, a living emotion.
In the heart of the Navarrese Pyrenees, in the lands of Roncesvalles, the Song of Roland was written. It was begun in the XI century and is the most celebrated heroic written in Romance language. The poem is based on the defeat suffered by the troops of Charlemagne against the Basque mountain people. Roland, who is the proud knight comprising all the virtues of a medieval hero, is too proud to ask for help. With his mouth bleeding copiously and his skull broken, he fights to the limits of his strenght. When at last he feels that everything is lost, he blows on his horn a few desperate notes. But it is too late. The prince dies amongst the remains of his army. His beloved Alda will cry for him in France. In the background of the song, the voice of the old emperor Charlemagne, who has seen the youngest and bravest men of his court die, says: "How painful is life, Lord!"
The history of Navarra could be told in this way, like a war song, with intense action and vivid adventure. Because of this the Navarrese are attached to tradition. When history has such a brave outline and sharp moments, it compels one to continue its example.
The Navarrese like to take life's risks, to experience the thrill of emotions. When the fiestas of San Fermin happen, in July, he runs in front of charging bulls. Why? Because when life is risked, just as when wine is drunk quickly, it has a stronger and more effective taste.
The Navarrese are naturally prone to taking risks, and discover in danger the potential for inmortality. "Their idea of honor is to allow themselves to be slaughtered by their foes," said one amazed Italian captain. "The man died but not his name," can be read in the coat of arms of a Navarrese nobleman. This is a firm philosophy best understood when experienced: a famous American author said that running in front of the bull in San Fermin was akin to getting baptized or becoming a Spanish citizen. This may be one of the most appealing experiences foreigners attempt when trying to feel Spanish.
The medieval tradition plays a large role in Navarrese behavior. For them life is noble only when taken lightly, and if hand in hand with this, one has religious convictions. These are, surely the same spiritual guidelines the pilgrims to St. James carried in their souls. The towns of St. Jean Pied de Port and Roncesvalles served as the earliest gateways to the roads of pilgrimage in all Spain. There is no doubt that the seeds of many Navarrese ideals were planted along this route, this road of faith and adventure.
The power of the church, being a universal institution, was always strong in Navarra, and the Catholic value system blended easily with the Navarrese way of life. During the civil wars that razed Spain in the XIX and XX centuries, a large number of young Navarrese men gave their lives in the name of their ideals. It would very simple, very easy, to judge this attitude from a prejudiced point of view, from this or that side of the game. But the Navarrese does not look at history horizontally, from the left or the right. His view of life is transcendent and vertical, with a high and a low point, just like that of the pilgrims of St. James, who walked across valleys singing psalms to the starry night.
Civil wars and the ruin of the Spanish Empire were severe blows for the Navarrese economy. The countryside was abandoned and an exodus from the towns to the cities took place. The Navarrese, however, faithfully preserved his ideals, always defending his rights and traditions in the most unfavorable circumstances. When he defends and claims his historic inheritance, he takes a strong stand. The heroic songs and Christian ideals of the Middle Ages were created in these lands: nothing less than the soul and spirit of Europe.

NAVARRE

Aerial view of Pamplona

City Hall of Pamplona

Estella

The Ebro River at Tudela

Plaza de los Fueros, Tudela

Castle of Javier

VALENCIA

To describe Valencia is like talking about certain artists, for the colors are immediately the main attraction: the multi-hued gardens, almond trees and "fallas" (huge cardboard statues). This vivid and Baroque image of the Valencian country can be seen in the lives and work of many Valencians, for instance an artist like Sorolla, a family like the Borgias or a writer like Vicente Blasco Ibañez. Rodrigo Borgia — his real name was Borja — is one of the most famous historical figures of Valencia. He was born in Xátiva, where he became renowned for his uglyness and the potence of his genitals. He began his religious career thanks to the influence of his uncle, the Pope Calixto III, who later gave Rodrigo access to the Vatican hierarchy. When the nephew became Pope, he took the name Alexandro VI and, when he died he left a cursed and feared progeny who have filled up chapters of world history with their names. These include the murderer Ceasar and the poisoner Lucrecia Borgia, both children of that fierce Valencian man. History told so sketchly is gory; but the man of Valencia — do not be scared! — is a natural biographer and writer. He knows how to point out the unusual, that which stands out for better or for worse, in life.

"Something must be in the water, that it is blessed" says a Castilian proverb. And something of truth must indeed be in Valencia that it is so dense and so Baroque.

> Valencia
> is the land of flowers,
> of light and color.

No one can remove from Valencia this image of pasodoble dance and fiesta. Even tourists know this easy and happy song by heart, written by the composer Padilla, which became famous during the 1930's. And so one is not to blame if the Valencian is always thought of this way, in custome. Neither will be the Valencian offended by this kind misconception of his land.

If Valencia were a Spanish souvenir, it would have always been the one most heavily exported. It has been like a display case for all Spain, showing the choicest of its products. From Valencia come oranges, the pasodoble dance and the paella. The man of Valencia is used to exporting the most regional things to a vast international market. Most of the products "Made in Spain" are really "Made in Valencia." In this world that is busy exporting terrible weapons, dangerous forms of

energy, and intangible ideals, Valencia specializes in sending out pasodobles, paella, oranges, toys, shoes and colorful biographies, like the history of Rodrigo Borgia. When Spaniards travel to Europe they want to forget about their "black legend" — the Inquisition, dictators, the abuses of the Spanish Empire — and just set up the Valencian display case which amounts to forgiveness for all our sins. "Aren't you still killing heretics?"
"No señor, now we are exporting sour oranges; it is almost the same thing."

I think, that in the end, the Baroque misconception of Valencia is a work done by Valencians themselves. The average Levantine soul has a special talent for grasping overstatement, wordiness and other kinds of excess. When this soul expresses itself humorously, it produces the "fallas," and when acts dramatically, it gives us tragedy or Expresionism. The popular artists who build the "fallas" are nothing but sculptors of caricature. They swell and exaggerate expression in their huge cardboard dolls, just as a journalist exaggerates his headlines in order to give his news shape, a concrete outline.

Inside the external colors of Valencia one finds at times an internal, bitter pesimism. On the outside one sees villages painted in blue, or pink or green, like a carnival. If one desires to look deeper into the Valencian soul, one must look past the color, past the spectrum of light. Do not forget that this is a land always in close contact with the sun, in other words, used to playing with mirages. "I would not be able to live in those countries of pale colors," said the painter Sorolla.

So what about the ancient Valencians? Those who, as legend goes, burned to death among the ruins of Sagunto rather than surrendering to the Romans; or what about the Valencians who sculpted the renowned Dama de Elche; or the descendants of the Iberian Romans, Goths and Arabs...? Most of today's Valencians are descended from Catalonian and Aragonese settlers who colonized Valencia in the XIII century. Any records of earliest history were lost when King Felipe III expelled the Muslims from Spain by royal decree in 1609. Valencia, the land of naked landscapes, mud and cane and growing rice; also a land of the huge palm groves of Elche, a whitewashed Moorish city surrounded by date-grows. Valencia, too, has orange groves as vast as the Ganges river valley, and the beautiful beaches of Alicante and Benidorm... It has bee said that this is the land of flowers, lights and color... It could be that it is true.

CASTELLON
Plaza Mayor and Tower of the
Cathedral

Peñiscola

Albocacer

Lucena del Cid

Castle of Chivert

Morella

VALENCIA

Santa Catalina

"Las Fallas" fiesta

Tower of Serranos

Plaza del Caudillo

La Albufera

Roman theater,
Sagunto

Cullera

Gandía

CANTE

v over the old downtown
a and commercial port

idorm

idorm

a

e

n-tree grove at
e

Lady of Elche

le of Guadelest

PAIS VASCO

Spain has always loved ideals more than nature. But there is one area of exception which lets man feel like lord of the forests: I am obviously talking about the Basque country. The Basque temperament is naturally superstitious, pagan, archaic and mountain oriented. Basque is a living blood which withstands the cold divisions of history or chronology. One is born Basque just like an oak tree or a mountain is: according to the laws of nature. And once born Basque one is a part of nature, united to the trees and the valleys by the mysterious bonds of kinship and love. That is what the learned call a pagan spirit. But this is not the civilized Latin paganism that turns gods into sedentary, old and burgoise senators or Roman patricians. The Basque paganism includes communication with trees and forest genies. A very mysterious, brave and ancient paganism. It is so mysterious and ancient that there is always an idiot ready to prove that the man of Neanderthal was Basque or that the "eusquera" language was spoken by Adam in Paradise.

All things are ancient in the Basque country, like nature itself; and mysterious like a river, a mountain, a cloud or the ocean. They are not officially "archeological" or intelectualized, because the Basques laugh at any degree of pretension or categorizing, no matter how important, and even scoff at history.

The Basques have made many important historical contributions, but have written few books and spread little news unlike others more inclined to chronicling. The peasants who defeated Charlemagne in Roncesvalles, under a shower of rocks, were Basques. However, there is no historical prove whatsoever that it was they who won the battle. The French wrote the Song of Roland, and Castilians created the legend of the Carpio. The Basque people forgot their own history. Another Basque was Iradier, the composer of many popular XIX century Spanish songs, and the man who inspired Bizet to create his famous Carmen opera. Iradier was also the singing teacher for the Empress Eugenia de Montijo. He is one of the greatest Basque artists and perhaps being Basque was the explanation for his fall into musical oblivion. The first Spanish encyclopedists as well as Juan Sebastian de Elcano — the man who accompanied Magallanes around the world — were Basque. When de Elcano returned from his voyage, King Carlos V bestowed upon him the honor of attaching a terrestrial globe with the inscription: "Primus

circumdedisti me" (first circumscribed by me) to his coat of arms. He was later relegated to a second captain of a ship.

The notable absence of Basque names in history is a mysterious thing. When they do enter in the pages of history as sailors, or soldiers, or men of achievements, they enter in groups, or species, as part of a society.

"Who won the Battle of Roncesvalles?"

"The Basques."

Linked to Spain and France by physical bonds, the people of Basque sometimes feel lost between these two countries who worship individual glory and fame. And then one sees the contradiction: the Basque pride in their houses adorned with coats of arms, indicating a strong attachment to family names. This is also seen in the ferocious characters — Baroja, Unamuno, Arazandi, — who have voiced the most honest and passionate criticism of Spain. No one in Spain took heed of the wise anthropologist Arazandi while he lived. But he took revenge in his own way while teaching his university class. Pacing up and down with his ungraceful limp, he said to his pupils:

"Culture in Spain limps like I do..."

The Basque is a frontier man, accustomed to seeing Spain in perspective and so, able to judge it at a distance. He loves Spain accordingly with the passion described in the poems of Iparraguirre, the man who composed the inmortal stanzas of the "Guernicaco Arbola" (the tree of Guernica).

Ara nun diran mendi maiteac
Ara nun diran celayac.
Bazerri eder, zurizuriyac
Iturri eta ibayac
Handayan nago zoraturican
Zabal zabalic beguira.
Ara España, lur oberican
Ez da Europa gustian.

There it is our beloved mountain,
there it is the meadow.
The white, very white country houses
the fountain and the river.
I'm here in Hendaya growing mad,
with my eyes wide open, looking.
There it is Spain, a better land
does not exist in Europe.

When a Basque looks at Spain he sees it with Basque eyes; searching for its rustic village houses,

trees, mountains, springs and rivers. He does not look to see its ideas or monuments or history. He loves his country with the almost Franciscan tenderness of a people used to looking at Nature. Voltaire said with much wit that the Basques are people who dance in the Pyrenees. The muse of Dionisus, the spirit of dance, is not foreign to those people who live in the valleys and who have placed their gods on the tops of mountains. They have never originated a classical culture. They belong to Nature, the mountains, the wind and their songs. To survive in a world which puts little stock in Nature, the Basques have created the heaviest industry in Spain; they have to move among fumes and cranes, bridges and blast furnaces. But in the depth of that industrial smog they sadly dream of the sweet smell of their mountains, the scent of hay, the fragrance of moisted meadows, the silvered leaves, the fireplace at home and the thick woods that nest flocks of singing birds.

ALAVA

Plaza de España
and Cathedral of
Vitoria

Plaza de España,
Vitoria

BISCAY

Santurce

Aerial view of
the port and
shipyards of
Bilbao

Portugalete

The Tree of
Guernica

GUIPUZCOA

San Sebastián

GUIPUZCOA

Partial view of La Concha,
San Sebastián

Fishing port, San Sebastián

Yacht-harbor, San Sebastián

Fishing port, Guelaria

Fishing port, Pasajes

Fishing port, Motrico

ISLAS BALEARES

Islands are traditionally literary, romantic and unique. They suffer a reputation manufactured in travel agencies for tourists feeling like disciples of Robinson Crusoe. The Balearic Islands prove the myth wrong, for they have always been centers of trade and culture. Greeks, Romans, Carthaginians, Arabs and most civilized cultures in history stopped at their ports. One of the great figures of the Islands, Raimon Llull, born in Majorca, was a theologist, poet, philosopher and scientist, and wrote his books in Catalan, Latin and Arabic. He reminds us of a Renaissance humanist genius; even his interest in astrology clearly belongs to the Renaissance. The Balearic man does not have a conqueror's will; when he sails out to sea, he brings no army, weapons or warships. He is guided by his companions, the stars and the sun and memories of the matchless light and calm nights of his land. It is obvious, therefore, that the Balearic Islands have produced scores of cartographers and explorers, never mentioned in the history of empires but known in the annals of common knowledge. "What would you ask me if I doubled your sufferings?" asks a character in one of Llull's works. "To double my love instead," answers the other one.

This is where the hidden treasure of these Islands lies: in the men who become enlightened with the patient cultivation of land, in the daily adventure of the harvests and in navegation. Consider that even the vegetation attains here — we are in the classical Mediterranean sea! — a human dimension. The olive tree reaches human heights and the almond tree has the shape of a woman when it blossoms in winter.

There is humanity to the olive tree, that when squeezed by civilization and culture, it gives the soft and slippery wisdom of its oil. The most diverse races and ideas blend perfectly in these islands, for the Balearics make up a bridge between Europe and Africa, and between the classical measure of the ancient Greeks and the Baroque disdain of the Arabic dance.

Each of the islands — Majorca, Menorca, Ibiza, Formentera, Cabrera —, has its own profile; only recently was communication between them made easy. Each island has its own distinctive dialect derived from Catalan. The language has aged over a long time, like a handicraft of mind and life. This could not be more different from life according to Robinson Crusoe. Here we have cultivated fields, history and high culture, evidenced by olive trees and cathedrals, almond trees and windmills, pine trees and Baroque furniture. Life passes on the Islands at the serene rhythm of a minuet, calm and noble like the "ball" for the peasants.

Perhaps this is the reason for the tourist "boom," coming from everywhere in the world every year. New hotels, appartment buildings, airports and shopping centers are constructed. Houses are better equiped for the needs of hospitality. But life's pace does not change and the tourist is soon caught up in its calm measure, the peace of a seaman who has experienced the soothing rocking of the waves.

MALLORCA
Port
Windmills at Palma de Majorca
Cala Figuera
Formentor
IBIZA
Port

Typical dance in Sa

San Antonio

MENORCA

Mahon

Mahon

Citadel

Rafalet Cove

Megalithic
monument in the
"Talatí de Dalt"

Benibeca

ISLAS CANARIAS

The Canary Islands have a dramatic and very beautiful legend. Like ancient goddesses they were born from the sea and the fire, from the volcano and the water. "Fortunate Islands," they were called by the first navigators. Are they perhaps the last survivors of that lost continent, the legendary Atlantis, sunk into the ocean?

When we watch them from the air we see the magical genesis of the archipielago. On one hand the destructive work of the waters and the erosion of the winds, on the other hand, the constructive, reinforcing, almost artisan work of the volcanoes. It is said that the first inhabitants of the islands came from the continent. The primitive "guanches" were shepherds, and carved their weapons out of the wood because they lacked knowledge of metals. With wheat and barley they prepared a kind of flour — gofio — that even today is a regional speciality of the Islands.

When the Islands were occupied by Spain during the Renaissance, they became part of Europe. People who came from Spain and from the continent — — Sevillans, Basques, Genoese, Portuguese — originated the blend of bloods which became the Island type. At times one sees descendants of the original "guanche" with his white hair and clear light eyes. This would be as common as seeing a descendant of the Phoenicians, Greeks or Romans on the continent. This is not a myth of folklore, but a fact of family, culture and assimilation.

Due to their geographical situation, the Canary Islands became early on a bridge for three continents: Europe, Africa and America. Because of this, they developed their ports, universities and trade skills. Some countries have colonized India, America or Africa. The people of the Canary Islands colonized the ocean. They placed themselves in the middle of the ocean like a lighthouse, as a reference of civilization open to trade and the interchange of ideas.

But the Canary Islands are not only a garden created by volcanoes and winds. These lands, seemingly soft and generous, have been opened to agriculture thanks to much patient effort. The Islands have a larger rural population than urban. Therefore the history of the Islands is still told from the countryside, from the little villages watching the crops, from men who cultivated the land by working their ploughs.

The Canarian is a man accustomed to patient toil. He works with the sensibility of an artisan and the precision of a goldsmith. Tilling the land, the farmer seems to be combing or drawing it. When the Corpus fiestas arrive, the streets are paved with flowers. And when working their crafts, the Canarians do delicate embroidery out of thread or palm fronds.

It is hard to find water on the Canary Islands. Sometimes it is necessary to drill tunnels and underground channels. This is almost work of inspiration, like the art of the waterwitch searching for water with the aid of a divining rod. So the most fertile soil has to be transported using man made resources, to the drier places.

Thanks to this skillful dedication, the Islands seem like a garden. But in some corners the dramatic images of bare rocks, deserts, or desolate lava can be seen. The foreign tourist is warmly drawn to this bright scenary mixing bananas and eucalyptus, red bougainvillea and the sea, palm trees and volcanoes.

The Canary Islands are, beyond a doubt, the dream of Europe: wonderful climate, exciting beaches and exotic gardens. But all this surrounded by an ancient culture discouraging wild folklore or safaris. I think the Canary Island are the sum of all the paradise imagined by Socrates, Goethe and Leonardo da Vinci. Herein lies their secret.

Guanche caves
(Gran Canaria)

General view of Las
Palmas

Provincial Museum of Fine
Arts, Las Palmas

General view of Las Palmas

Hostal of Santa
Cruz de Tenerife,
Gran Canaria

Tejeda, Gran
Canaria

Banana plantation
and panoramic
view of Lairaja,
Gran Canaria

Puerto de la Cr
Santa Cruz de
Tenerife

Puerto de la Cr
Santa Cruz de
Tenerife

A remarkable v
of Tenerife

Plaza de España, Santa Cruz de Tenerife

Easter Flower

Teide Peak, Santa Cruz de Tenerife

CEUTA

The bright, Andalusian city of Ceuta is positioned high over a narrow isthmus on the outskirts of Mount Acho. Its modern port offers good shelter to ships. Ceuta presents the lively, unmistakable profile of Mediterranean cities, as its history is linked to European culture from Greek and Roman times. By reason of its being a Free Tax Port, Ceuta is a busy, active city and a port for ferries linking Europe and Africa.

MELILLA

Melilla is one of the oldest European settlements on the African coast. It still retains memories of its past, but Melilla is above all a town with a modern, Mediterranean appearance. It enjoys a picturesque view over the Mediterranean as it is placed on the tip of a peninsula.

Fire Mountain, Lanzarote

Typical architecture at Icod de los Vinos

Windmill, Lanzarote

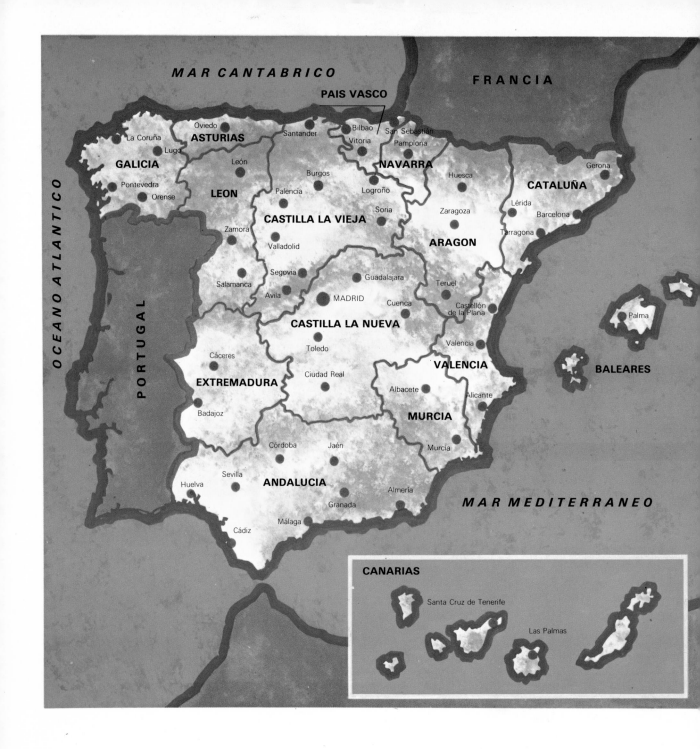

ICONOGRAPHY - SALMER, GEOCOLOR, FIRO FOTO, ROTGER, CANÓS.

Printed in Spain  GEOCOLOR®

COGRAF,S.A. Dep. Leg. · B · 12.384 · 79